MADAM SECRETARY
The Story of Madeleine Albright

Notable Americans

MADAM SECRETARY
The Story of Madeleine Albright

Jeremy Byman

MORGAN REYNOLDS Incorporated

Greensboro

MADAM SECRETARY: *The Story of Madeleine Albright*

Copyright © 1998 by Jeremy Byman

Photo credits: AP/World Wide Photos; Chicago Sun Times, Wellesley College; Sygma;
Kent-Denver School.

Library of Congress Cataloging-in-Publication Data
Byman, Jeremy, 1944-
   Madam secretary : the story of Madeleine Albright / Jeremy Byman. —1st ed.
      p. cm. — (Notable Americans)
   Includes bibliographical references and index.
   Summary: Focuses on the career of the former United States ambassador to the United
Nations who became the first woman to serve as Secretary of State.
   ISBN 1-883846-23-4
      1. Albright, Madeleine Korbel—Juvenile literature. 2. Women cabinet officers—
United States—Biography—Juvenile literature. 3. Cabinet officers—United States—
Biography—Juvenile literature. 4. United Nations—Officials and employees—Biogra-
phy—Juvenile literature. 5. Ambassadors—United States—Biography—Juvenile literature.
[1. Albright, Madeleine Korbel. 2. Women cabinet officers. 3. Cabinet officers.
4. Women ambassadors. 5. Ambassadors. 6. Women—Biography] I. Title II. Series.
E840.8.A37B96 1997
327.73'0092—dc21

                                                                              97-38397
                                                                              CIP

Printed in the United States of America
First Edition

To Lynn—
for all her encouragement

Contents

Madeleine Albright

Chapter One

Flee or Die

Thursday, February 20, 1997, had been a tiring day for Madeleine Albright. It was late when she finally sat down in front of a computer in Moscow's American Center. The new secretary of state had spent the day negotiating with the Russians. They were discussing America's plan to let the former allies of the old Soviet Union join the North Atlantic Treaty Organization (NATO). Russia was opposed to the plan and had promised some form of diplomatic retaliation if the changes were made.

Madeleine's day had been long, but it was not yet over. She had promised to be the first secretary of state to host a chat room on the World Wide Web. She was going to talk with students from 3,000 schools in the United States, including the high school she had attended in Denver, as well as the rest of the world. Although she was tired, this looked to be more fun than arguing with the Russians.

Madeleine began the session by telling the students a little about her last few days. "I just finished dinner with the Russian foreign minister—caviar and sturgeon, with Russian blini, a wonderful but fattening dinner.

"I left Washington on Saturday and landed in Rome that night. I met with the leaders of Italy on Sunday and have since flown to France, Germany, and the United Kingdom. On the way, I stopped off in Brussels, Belgium, where I made a speech to the foreign ministers of all the NATO alliance countries. Today I met with the prime minister and foreign minister of Russia and will meet with President Yeltsin tomorrow. After that I will fly on to Seoul, Tokyo, and Beijing. Nine cities in ten days! I am halfway through my trip."

Then it was time for the questions. Madeleine soon discovered that the students had been paying attention to the news.

"How would the recent death of China's ruler affect America's relations with that country?"

"What could the U.S. do to make the Mexican economy stronger?"

"What would happen to Hong Kong when China took it over that summer?"

Some of the questions were more personal.

"Do you feel special about being the first woman to be secretary of state?"

"Do you think your gender will create problems for you in dealing with countries that don't allow women in positions of authority and leadership?"

Madeleine met with Russian Prime Minister Vicktor Chernomyrdin in February 1997 to discuss the future expansion of NATO.

To this last question Madeleine answered that she did not think her gender would be a problem. "Even in countries that do not have women in high level positions, they do want to deal with the United States. And so I think that I will be respected because I represent the most wonderful and influential country in the world. It would be nice, however, if there were more women in high level positions."

Madeleine received several questions from Czechoslovakia, the land of her birth. She answered these in both English and Czech.

Then a second grader in Ada, Oklahoma, asked a question Madeleine had answered several times in the past days. "Were you surprised to find out that you were Jewish?"

"Yes," Madeleine said. She had been brought up to believe she was Catholic. Madeleine knew, of course, that her family had fled Czechoslovakia when the Nazis came to power, when she was a small child. And there had been rumors that her family had been Jewish before converting to Catholicism. But this had been confirmed only recently, in the rush of press attention brought on by her appointment as the first female secretary of state.

Another student from Oklahoma wanted to know if she liked the name "Madeleine." Secretary Albright did not tell the student that she was not even sure what her original name was. Some of her family said that her given name was "Madeleine Jane," others say it was "Maria Jana" or "Marie Jana," and that one of her grandmothers nicknamed her

"Madlenka." Her name did not permanently become "Madeleine" until she was ten.

The girl who became known as Madeleine Korbel was born in a confusing time, on May 15, 1937, and in a confusing place, Prague, the capital of Czechoslovakia. It was a country struggling to survive under the shadow of a brutal northern neighbor, Nazi Germany. Her father, Josef, was a rising star in the Czech diplomatic service. She was the oldest child. Eventually her mother, Mandula, had two more children, Anna Katherine (called Kathy) and John Joseph.

Josef Korbel loved the Czechoslovak state he served. The country had been born out of the destruction of war. He later described his country as rising "phoenix-like from the ashes of the Austro-Hungarian empire," the vast European state shattered by its defeat in World War I. What was most important to him was that Czechoslovakia welcomed many different ethnic and religious groups, including Czechs, Germans, Slovaks, Magyars (Hungarians) and Jews. To Josef, this diversity symbolized the progress and freedom his own family had enjoyed as they had prospered in the building supply business.

By 1937 the Nazis threatened to end the liberal traditions of Josef's beloved country. The Korbels had special reason to fear the Nazis. The family was Jewish, and the Nazis had made it clear that they hated Jews. That hatred would eventually result in the killing of six million Jews.

What was new about the Nazis was not their hatred for the Jews, but the huge design of their murderous plans. Jews had been the target of prejudice and hatred in Europe for centuries. In the part of the Austro-Hungarian empire that eventually become Czechoslovakia, there had been horrifying assaults on Jews. In 1897, a "pogrom"—an attack carried out by private citizens—raged in Prague for three days. Mobs looted Jewish-owned shops and businesses, ransacked synagogues, and assaulted or killed anyone who seemed to be a Jew. Order was established only after the government declared martial law and brought troops into Prague.

Two years later, in 1899, only 10 years before Josef Korbel's birth, a Jewish shoemaker, Leopold Hilsner, and the entire Jewish community of Polna were accused of ritual murder. Another pogrom and a flood of anti-Semitic propaganda followed.

The Jews of Czechoslovakia knew how easily they could be hated and subjected to physical and verbal abuse. As Madeleine's mother said to a family friend, "To be a Jew is to be constantly threatened by some kind of danger. That is our history."

The Korbel family did not live as Jews. They thought of themselves primarily as Czechs. With their connection to their religion so slight, and their Czech nationalism so sincere, what they had to do seemed obvious to them. The way to escape anti-Semitism was to officially stop being

Jews by converting to Catholicism, the dominant religion in Czechoslovakia.

The problem in the late 1930s was that, according to the twisted Nazis ideology, "once a Jew, always a Jew." Or, as Dagmar Sima, Madeleine's cousin, puts it, "The only sense in which we were Jews was under the definition of . . . Hitler and the Nazis." Clearly, despite the Korbel family conversion, they had much to fear from the Nazis.

Josef had been appointed to serve at the Czech embassy in Belgrade, Yugoslavia, soon after Madeleine was born. Two years later he was recalled to Prague, just as the Munich Pact between Germany and Britain placed Czechoslovakia's future in the hands of the Nazis.

Shortly after returning to Prague, it became clear to Josef that the people identified as Jews had two choices. They could flee or die. He began making plans to flee.

After returning from a diplomatic assignment in Britain only two days before the Nazi takeover of his country, Josef knew he had to act quickly. In an eleven page family history written thirty years after the war, Mandula Korbel described her flight from Czechoslovakia with Josef and the two-year-old Madeleine, ten days after the Nazis arrived in 1939.

In the days before escaping, Josef and Mandula walked the streets of Prague with their baby daughter in their arms. They were careful to stay in public places until they got fake diplomatic papers. Banks were closed, Mandula wrote. "Friends were being arrested. Josef's name was on a list of people [who were being hunted by the Nazis]. With the help of some good friends and lots of luck and a little bribery, we managed to get the necessary Gestapo [secret police] permission to leave the country."

Saying a hasty goodbye to family and friends, the Korbels escaped before the Germans were able to seal the border. They fled to London. "That was the last time we saw our parents alive," wrote Madeleine's mother.

The family's flight was frightening. But it was also the kind of major life change that Josef and Mandula had grown used too and would experience more often in the future. As a member of the Czech diplomatic service, he had always needed to be ready to live anywhere in the world to represent his country. Since Madeleine's birth, the Korbel family had lived in Prague and Belgrade. Now came London. Madeleine said years later, "I made friends very easily. I think it has to do with the fact that I lived in a lot of different countries, went to a lot of different schools and was always being put into situations where I had to relate to the people around me."

It was as though Madeleine was being trained as a diplomat from birth. In fact, on more than a few occasions during those years, Madeleine would find herself acting the part of the diplomat. Her father would recruit her to present bouquets to visiting dignitaries during welcoming ceremonies. She did it so often that she soon became known as "the little blond girl in the national costume."

While living in London during World War II, Madeleine (right) often wore traditional Czech costume.

There was also a fascination with the only religion she knew. "As a child I was a very serious Catholic." She loved the Virgin Mary and "played a priest—I was already playing male roles."

The Korbels stayed in London through World War II. Josef worked for the exiled Czechoslovak government as an aide to the Czech foreign minister, Jan Masaryk. Josef's was one of many voices from around the world heard on the British Broadcasting Corporation, the government's worldwide radio service. It sent news and messages of hope to people living under the Nazi dictatorship.

The war years in London made a big impression on Madeleine. In an interview after becoming secretary of state, she said: "I remember the war distinctly. We were in London during the blitz. I remember what it was like to come out of the air-raid shelter and see London bombed. I remember spending huge portions of my life in air-raid shelters singing 'A Hundred Green Bottles Hanging On the Wall.' I remember when we moved to Walton-on-Thames, where they had just invented some kind of a steel table. They said if your house was bombed and you were under the table, you would survive. We had this table, and we ate on the table and we slept under the table and we played around the table."

Madeleine's cousin Dagmar joined them in London. Dagmar was nine years older than Madeleine, who saw her as "a loved older cousin, looked up to as older cousins are."

Madeleine easily became fluent in English. She spoke with a Cockney accent, just like many of the English people she lived among. Eventually, she lost her Czech accent entirely.

It was also during this time that she began to learn about politics and develop the understanding of the world that would influence her thinking as an adult. Much of this insight came from listening to her parents tell stories of what Czechoslovakia was like between the wars. In the minds of her father and mother, it was hard to distinguish between the Korbel family history and the history of Czechoslovakia. They told her about their childhood holidays and other pleasant memories. "Mostly," she says, "they spoke of politics, about how the period between the world wars was a golden time for Czechoslovakia. My parents had been in their twenties and he was a diplomat, and they talked more about being the first generation of adults in free Czechoslovakia. This was their pride and this is what I grew up with."

Her parents' memories were like fairy tales that made sense to a five-year-old, in the way that stories about "olden times" often do. "I had a story and there were no gaps in the story. And as a child, if there are no gaps, you don't ask questions." She didn't remember her grandparents in Prague, though she was told she had stayed with them when she was only a year old. "I had no actual knowledge of them. When people are not a visible part of your life, you don't ask about them," she remembered later.

Then the wonderful day came when seven-year-old Madeleine sat glued to a radio in London. She was listening, with her father, to news of the U.S. Army's liberation of the western part of her native land. They cheered when General George Patton's troops forced Nazi soldiers out of the famous brewery town of Pilsen. They worried when Patton was forced to hold back his troops and let the Soviet Red Army capture Prague as arranged between the Americans, British, and Soviets months before. "I remember the broadcasts as the Nazis were pushed back across Czechoslovakia, and I remember my parents cheering and wishing they had gone further," she told hundreds of American and Czech veterans in Pilsen a half century later.

When the war ended in May of 1945, the Korbels returned to Prague—and Josef and Mandula discovered to their horror that those who had stayed were all gone. Madeleine's paternal grandparents, Arnost and Olga Korbel, had died at Auschwitz. The Nazis had also killed her maternal grandmother, Anna Speiglovna, and a dozen of her relatives. Cousin Dagmar had lost her parents and sister and many of her other relatives. According to Dagmar, Madeleine, who was only eight years old, was considered too young to be told the true story of how the Nazis had destroyed her extended family.

Dagmar continued to stay with the Korbels, this time in

Belgrade, where Josef was serving as the Czech ambassador. It was time for Madeleine to begin school. Because her parents were opposed to dictatorship of any kind, they did not want her to come under the influence of the communists who controlled the schools in Yugoslavia. They arranged for her to be tutored at home. When she was ten, she was sent to a boarding school in Switzerland, where she learned French—and where she began to be called "Madeleine."

The early months of 1948 were another period of great anxiety for the Korbels. In February the Czech government was overthrown by the communists, the very people Josef had come to fear. Soon after the takeover, Josef's friend and mentor, Foreign Minister Jan Masaryk, fell, jumped, or was pushed to his death from a high window of the Foreign Ministry building. Josef thought Masaryk's death easily explained: "He was murdered by Soviet agents," he said. The death devastated him. He returned to Prague from Belgrade for the funeral. It was the last time he saw his home.

After returning to Belgrade, Josef learned that the new communist government had charged him with crimes against the state "in absentia,"which meant he had not been present to defend himself. One of his colleagues, who was himself imprisoned for thirteen years, remembers that "Sooner or later Josef would have been imprisoned. The question at the time was, [was Josef] a democrat or not. He was very dangerous to the communists." Nearly two hundred of

Josef's colleagues were arrested and executed.

The family, still in Belgrade, endured several months of uncertainty. Madeleine finished the school year in Switzerland and returned to Belgrade. After her return, Josef sent a cable to Prague announcing he was leaving for vacation with his family. To fool the communists about their true intentions, the Korbels sent their household possessions back to Prague. They then boarded a train for London, and from there a boat for New York. Josef was quickly granted temporary political refugee status.

Dagmar remained in Prague. Divided by the "Iron Curtain," the border between the communist and democratic countries, the cousins continued to write to each other. They would not see each other again for forty years, when communist control of Czechoslovakia ended in 1989.

The Korbels were soon granted permanent political asylum in the United States—meaning that the government had decided that their lives were in danger if they returned to their native country. Eleven-year-old Madeleine Korbel had finally arrived at a permanent home.

Chapter Two

New World

When Madeleine arrived in the United States, she was only eleven, but she had already lived in four countries. She and her family had been made refugees twice—first by the Nazis, and now by the communists. The Korbels, like many other immigrant Americans, would "close the book" on the pre-American chapter of their lives, turning their back on that sad period and starting a new life. They looked only to the future from then. Madeleine has never questioned the choices made by her parents, whom she called "the bravest people alive." But one thing was certain: The experience of escaping from murderous governments affected her thinking profoundly.

The family moved to Colorado in 1949—driving across country in a little green Ford coupe—after her father was appointed professor of international relations at the University of Denver. He was beginning a highly successful career in academia and soon earned a permanent appointment at the university. In the next years he gained wide respect by writing many books on foreign affairs and on Central and Eastern Europe.

Later, during the 1960s, Josef became well-known for his fervent defense of America's involvement in Vietnam. He maintained this position even after the war became highly unpopular, especially on college campuses. For him the war was simply a struggle against communist expansion. This greatly influenced Madeleine's strategic thinking. Eventually, Josef became dean of the Graduate School of International Studies at the University of Denver.

Curiously, in one of his books, *The Communist Subversion of Czechoslovakia (1938-1948)*, Josef attacked what the Nazis had done to Czechoslovakia—killing leaders, destroying the native culture and the national economy, and closing universities. But, he did not mention what had happened to more than 100,000 Jews in his homeland, most of whom, like his mother and father, were killed by the Nazis.

The Korbels lived in a small apartment near downtown Denver, in housing provided for University of Denver faculty. Needing quiet, and privacy, Madeleine went daily to the library to study. "I spent a lot of time in libraries when I was in school," she remembers.

In their new lives, the Korbels remained Catholics. America was not Nazi Germany, but there were people who did not like Jews. During these years, many of the best colleges limited the number of Jews they would accept as students, and the "best" country clubs usually excluded them. Madeleine continued to grow up Catholic.

From her earliest years in school, Madeleine was a serious student. Her self-discipline and determination came from her father. Josef Korbel was a very old-fashioned, formal man. He was so formal, in fact, that he had learned to ski while wearing a topcoat and tie. "He was a strict European parent," says younger brother John. Family routines were sacrosanct. Children were expected to be at the dinner table on time. "The most severe form of punishment was when our father wouldn't talk to us for a week," John says.

Madeleine often mentions her father and his scholarly writings in her speeches, and during interviews she has placed his name at the top of her list of mentors. By her own account, her worldview consists largely of ideas he "implanted" in her. She often heard her father sharing his ideas with university students who visited the Korbel home. During these visits, her mother made people feel welcome and did palm readings for fun. Her father was an inspirational figure to the students, "a great intellectual humanist," Madeleine remembers.

Madeleine adjusted quickly to life in America. She jokes that she soon became "thoroughly American Madeleine." But her modern thinking and Josef's old world ways did occasionally come into conflict. She still remembers one such disagreement when she was invited to the prom in the ninth grade, and her father did not want her riding without a chaperone in a boy's car. After much discussion, Josef came up with a "compromise." She rode to the prom with her date, and Josef followed in his car. When the dance ended, Josef drove Madeleine home. "To this day, I will never forget the mortification—when he made me get into his car while my date followed me home, then invited this poor boy in for milk and cookies," she remembered years later. "I didn't see that boy again."

It was not their only conflict. Madeleine wanted to go to the nearby public high school. Josef insisted she enroll at Kent Denver School, a small private high school for girls in nearby Englewood, Colorado, that had offered her a scholarship. This disagreement led to the only heated confrontation with her father that Madeleine can recall. Josef won the argument, and today Madeleine admits that he was probably right. "The Kent School did give me a tremendous education. I was pretty serious. I think I was pretty boring in high school. I was a foreign policy wonk even then." Fellow classmates, when asked about her decades later, say she was always a leader. "She ran everything," said one, adding quickly, "But she wasn't bossy."

At Kent Denver School, Madeleine founded an international relations club, appointing herself its president. "I

Madeleine's father insisted she attend Kent Denver School, a private high school for girls.

Madeleine founded the Kent Denver International Relations Club.

tortured my classmates and made them come to meetings," she told more than 600 people gathered in a campus hall on a visit to her old school in May 1997. "I won the United Nations contest because I memorized, alphabetically, all fifty-one countries that were U.N. members. I couldn't do that now. There are 185 members."

There is a simple wooden sign near the entrance to her old high school that reads "Kent Denver School." A few feet beyond is another, matching sign: "Madeleine Albright. Secretary of State. Class of 1955."

In the fall of 1955 Madeleine entered Wellesley College, in Wellesley, Massachusetts, a distinguished women's college that had granted her a scholarship. She continued to work hard at college and developed organizational skills that still serve her to this day. She even organized her neatly underlined notes into fifteen different colored notebooks.

At Wellesley, Madeleine majored in political science. The academic demands were challenging, but she still found time to campaign for Adlai Stevenson, the Democratic candidate who lost to President Eisenhower in the 1956 presidential race. During the election year, she collected "dollars for Democrats" on Boston Common. She also edited the campus newspaper.

Madeleine did not work all the time while she was in college. One other useful skill she learned during these years was how to shop for discounts in Boston's famous Filene's department store basement.

MADELEINE KORBEL

International relations, Princeton, or any other topic brings forth a flood of comment from Madeleine, expert if on the first subject, and a bit incoherent if on the second. You will often find her taking a definite stand on matters, staunchly saying, "You guys, this just proves it!" Her constant interest in anything she is doing, and the drive with which she does it, keep all interested in the activities of our "emaciated" companion.

Madeleine graduated from Kent Denver in 1955.

During the summer of 1957, after her sophomore year, Madeleine interned at her hometown newspaper, the *Denver Post*. Her career goal was to graduate and work as a reporter. While at the *Post*, she wrote stories about weddings and worked in the morgue (back-issue file room).

Another intern was Joseph Medill Patterson Albright, a descendant of one of America's most famous newspaper-owning families. Joe's ancestor, Joseph Medill, had founded the *Chicago Tribune* and turned it into a national power in the years before the Civil War. Some say that Joseph Medill was the person most responsible for the election of Abraham Lincoln in 1860. Joe's grandfather, Joseph Patterson, started the *New York Daily News* in 1919, and his aunt, Alicia Patterson Guggenheim, founded *Newsday* on Long Island, outside of New York City, in 1940.

Joseph Albright was a quiet, private man who had graduated from Williams College. He was an heir to a great fortune earned in the profession Madeleine wanted to pursue. It seemed a perfect match. Soon, she and Joseph were dating. They began making plans for a future together.

If Madeleine had any questions about her family's religious heritage during her college years, she never expressed them publicly. One of her best friends at Wellesley was Emily Cohen MacFarquhar, who said that Madeleine never gave any hint that she had any doubt about her parents' account of their lives in Europe. "I've known her intimately for forty-one years and knew her parents very well, and I

Madeleine's career goal during college was to graduate and become a journalist.

know for absolute certainty that she knew nothing about it."

Madeleine graduated from Wellesley with honors in 1959—just a few years before her future "employer's" wife, Hillary Rodham Clinton, enrolled at the college. Her graduation commencement speaker told her class that their role in life was to raise the next generation of educated citizens.

While being a mother and wife was not Madeleine's only goal, it certainly was one that she prized highly. So it was no surprise to anyone when she married Joe Albright three days after graduation.

Chapter Three

Marriage

After marrying Joe Albright, Madeleine worked briefly on the *Daily News* in Rolla, Missouri. Then the couple moved to Chicago, where Joe got a job at the *Chicago Sun-Times*. Madeleine abandoned her own journalistic ambitions after their move, as the result of an interview she had with a *Sun-Times* editor. Calling her "honey," the editor told her that neither the *Sun-Times* nor its competitors would hire a spouse of a *Sun-Times* reporter because newspaper union rules barred it. He advised her to pursue another career.

Madeleine tried to see this gender prejudice in a positive light. "As it turns out, I was very lucky, because I would have been a lousy reporter, and I think I am pretty good at what I do now," she said later.

For a brief period in 1960, she held a job in public relations in the Chicago offices of Encyclopaedia Britannica. Then, in 1961, Joe took a job as a reporter and executive with *Newsday*, his aunt's newspaper, and the Albrights moved to Long Island.

Madeleine married Joe Albright three days after her college graduation.

After moving to New York, between 1961 and 1967 Madeleine gave birth to three daughters, the twins Anne and Alice, and then Katherine (called Katie), six years later. The twins were premature, and as a way of distracting herself from the stress of caring for two babies in incubators, she began to study Russian at Columbia University in New York City. As always, she was very efficient in the use of her time. While other people sat in movies just watching, she knitted sweaters.

When the twins were healthy, Madeleine hired a full-time housekeeper to help with child-care duties and enrolled in the graduate program in political science at Columbia.

Madeleine began attending graduate school while her twin daughters were infants.

Though she studied with many distinguished teachers, the one that would have the greatest influence on her future was Professor Zbigniew Brzezinski, an immigrant from Poland who at that time directed Columbia's Institute on Communist Affairs and later served as national security advisor during the Carter Administration.

Brzezinski was known for being a tough teacher. He wanted to make sure his students were committed to their studies. He rarely gave "A's," and when he did he attached a personal note of commendation. Madeleine was soon receiving these personal notes. It was in Brzezinski's classes that she realized she would have to do even better than the men if she were going to be taken seriously.

Because of her family responsibilities, it took until 1968 for Madeleine to earn a master of arts degree and a certificate in Russian studies, from Columbia. She then began doing research for her doctoral dissertation, a book-length study of a subject required before she could receive a Ph.D. degree. Her topic, the role of the press in the 1968 Czechoslovak democracy movement known as "The Prague Spring," also allowed her to use her native Czechoslovakian language. She focused on the role played by newspapers, TV and radio in the failed attempt to bring about democratic reforms in Czechoslovakia. In her research, she interviewed many dissidents who had participated in those events.

To meet her family obligations and also write the dissertation—which she described as "the hardest thing I ever did"—she got up every morning at 4:30. It took her eight more years after completing her master's degree to earn her Ph.D.

In those days it was much less common for a woman to be working full time and also taking care of a growing family. But her daughters did not feel ignored. Says Anne, "I always thought my mother's work was very exciting, and my sisters and I never felt that she didn't have enough time for us. She's always done the ordinary things that mothers do: getting us up in the mornings and ready for school, helping us with our homework. We used to do our home-

In 1968, Russian tanks brought an abrupt end to the brief period of freedom called the "Prague Spring".

work together. She was finishing her Ph.D., and we were in grade school. On Fridays she would do the grocery shopping while my sisters and I were horseback riding or taking ballet class or guitar lessons. We had a wonderful family life.

"She always taught us that being charming and attractive is not inconsistent with being smart and aggressive. But the real secret of her success is that she works like a dog. When we were children, my younger sister, Katie, wanted to be a fireman. My twin sister, Alice, wanted to be a doctor. I wanted to be a baseball player, a pitcher for the New York Mets. My mom never told us, you should do this or you should do that. Nevertheless, academic achievement was highly valued in our family and we were all history majors in college, like my father. Each of us sort of assumed we'd go to graduate school; we ended up as two lawyers and a banker. The one thing she really wanted to teach us was— do your best at your job, no matter what it is. She's said many times that there's no such thing as luck. What you get you work for."

"As kids," concludes Anne, "we never felt we were being sacrificed for her career. Quite the opposite."

Chapter Four

Washington Insider

In 1968 Joe was promoted to chief of *Newsday's* Washington bureau. This was an advance in his career, but it meant the family had to move to the nation's capital. For a while after arriving in Washington, Madeleine directed her considerable energy into volunteer activities, including serving on the board of directors of the Beauvoir School, a private school that the twins attended.

In the early 1970s, a fellow Beauvoir parent noted Madeleine's skill at raising money for the school. She suggested that Madeleine raise funds for Maine senator Edmund S. Muskie. He was seeking the 1972 Democratic presidential nomination. "She jumped right from fund raising for the kindergarten to fund raising for Muskie," recalls the friend.

Muskie did not win the 1972 presidential race. He remained a senator, however, and in 1976 he put Madeleine on his payroll as his chief legislative assistant. "I had just received my Ph.D. That made it possible for Senator Muskie to introduce me as Dr. Albright, instead of Madeleine Albright, little housewife," she jokes. The senator was a member of the Senate Foreign Relations Committee, and Madeleine spent a substantial portion of her time dealing with foreign affairs.

Senator Muskie was known for being smart but also demanding—and he had a temper. Woe be to the aide who didn't have the information he needed, when he needed it. But Professor Brzezinski had been much the same, so Madeleine was prepared to work for a tough boss.

It took a while for her daughters, who were young teens at the time, to understand all the ins and outs of work in the Congress. Once Anne wanted to get in touch with her mother. "When she went back to work, she told us we could call her at the office if anything ever came up. So we called one time when she was working for Senator Muskie, and the receptionist told us our mother couldn't come to the phone because she was on the floor with the senator. When she called back, we said, 'What were you doing on the floor with Senator Muskie?' She had been on the floor of the Senate, of course, but we were too young to know what she really did."

Madeleine's career moved forward steadily, and not just because she was a hard worker. She enjoyed the support of powerful men both in and out of government.

In 1978, Madeleine joined the staff of President Jimmy Carter's National Security Council, which advises the

Senator Edmund Muskie gave Madeleine her first job in government.

president on important foreign policy questions and deals with crises. She worked under her old professor Brzezinski, who was now President Carter's national security adviser. Madeleine served as a congressional liaison, focusing on foreign policy legislation. She had learned the delicate art of compromise, a critical skill in politics, and she was learning to make use of her natural charm.

Soon her negotiating skills became even more important, because Senator Muskie was now the secretary of state, and he did not always agree with Brzezinski. It would have been very easy to get caught in the crossfire between her two mentors. But she gracefully handled the tense situation. Says Brzezinski, "She kept me from getting in trouble with Congress." Others remembered that though she was in a relatively low-level staff job, "she was always at the center of things." Toward the end of her stay at the council, says Madeleine, Secretary Muskie made a clever joke about the fact that her mentors were both Polish-Americans: "Muskie said that I was unique in that I was the only woman in the world to go from Pole to Pole."

Madeleine learned some important lessons about women in politics during her days at the National Security Council. As a staff member, she "had to learn to speak out" for herself. "I would be in a White House meeting, and I would think of something and not say it because I wasn't sure that it would add to the discussion. Then some man would say

Madeleine served on President Jimmy Carter's National Security staff.

what I had been thinking, and it would be hailed as a great idea," she recalls.

When the Republican president, Ronald Reagan, took office in 1981, Madeleine had to leave the government. The new president gets to select people from his own party for the top jobs. She found a position as a researcher in Soviet and Eastern European affairs at the Center for Strategic and International Studies, one of the many "think tanks," or research centers, in Washington.

That same year she was awarded a fellowship at the Smithsonian Institution's Woodrow Wilson Center for Scholars. She worked on a book that dealt with many of the same questions she had looked at in her doctoral dissertation. It was published as *Poland: The Role of the Press in Political Change*.

The next year, 1982, saw big changes in Madeleine's life. Two of them were happy changes, toward which she had been working since she had first started studying Russian when her daughters were babies. The School of Foreign Service at Georgetown University appointed her to the dual positions of research professor of international affairs and director of the Women in Foreign Service Program.

She also began doing something that her father had done decades before in Denver, only she was doing it at a much higher level. She started hosting a kind of high-powered foreign policy salon in her home. She and her guests analyzed and debated current issues over dinner (usually a chicken-rice casserole, because it wasn't the food that was important). Through the years, these dinners included hundreds of Democratic politicians, professors and theoreticians. "These were not mere social gatherings, but sessions aimed at laying the groundwork for a Democratic return to power," according to one observer. Madeleine could improve her knowledge of foreign affairs while introducing herself and her ideas to people who would one day be in a position to make use of her talents.

But she was learning the ropes of international politics in more formal settings, too. She attended the Georgetown Leadership Seminar, which Henry Kissinger had created years before he became President Richard Nixon's secretary of state. Government officials, lawyers, bankers, journalists and military officers came from all over the world to listen for a week to policymakers from the State Department, the Pentagon, and foreign countries.

She also appeared regularly on the Public Broadcasting System television program "Great Decisions," which was run by her school. Though not many people tuned in to hear scholars and policymakers debate the foreign policy issues of the day, the people who did watch were important. The show provided her a chance to make an impression. She also ran the Center for National Policy, another "think tank."

Early in the same year that her public life began to

flourish her private life suffered a blow. As she later remembered that day in the living room of her Georgetown home, "It was January 13, 1982. At 8 o'clock in the morning and sitting on this very chair was Joe Albright, who said to me, 'This marriage is dead and I'm in love with somebody else.'"

Madeleine was stunned—she had had no idea that anything like this was coming. The divorce was finalized the next year, and Madeleine has not come close to remarrying since the breakup.

The divorce, which left her financially comfortable, including owership of a townhouse in the fashionable Georgetown section of Washington and a farm in Virginia, may also have left her stronger. "Our generation of women never expected this to happen to them," said a friend of hers. Although she has dated occasionally, Madeleine has not had a serious relationship since the divorce. For years Madeleine poured out her bitterness to friends, telling them that Joe Albright could not deal with a strong woman and that she never would have had much of a professional life if she had stayed married to him. Finally, several friends told her to shut up about Joe and get on with her life.

And she did.

Chapter Five

An Intellectual with a Heart

Madeleine made her political loyalties clear in 1956, when she campaigned for Democratic presidential candidate Adlai Stevenson against the highly popular Republican, President Eisenhower. She has remained a Democrat ever since. That means she works in the government only when Democrats win elections. When her candidates won, as Jimmy Carter did in 1976, she had a chance for a job in the administration. When they lost, she would have to go back to a job outside of government and wait for another campaign. During the 1980s, Democrats lost all three presidential campaigns to Republicans. But, no matter how devastating the defeats, she worked hard supporting a candidate in the next election. This persistence in the face of disappointments, which might have discouraged someone less dedicated, served her well in future years.

During the 1984 presidential race, Madeleine, while still teaching at Georgetown, served as the foreign policy coordinator for Walter Mondale, the Democratic candidate. And she worked for Mondale's running mate, Geraldine Ferraro, who was the first woman ever to run for vice president on a major party ticket. Ferraro was so determined to take advantage of Madeleine's foreign policy expertise that she taped her conversations and played them back later as she relaxed in her bath after a hard day's campaigning.

Later that year, after Mondale's loss to President Reagan in the November election, Madeleine found a way to keep herself and her ideas before Washington decision-makers. She became vice-chairperson of the National Democratic Institute for International Affairs, an organization that conducts nonpartisan international programs to help promote and strengthen democratic institutions.

Four years later, in 1988, it was time for another presidential election. Madeleine became Michael S. Dukakis's senior foreign policy adviser in the Massachusetts governor's campaign for the presidency. A few days after Dukakis's nomination at the 1988 Democratic National Convention, Madeleine described her role in his campaign. "The most important thing is not that he has my views but that he has information and I serve as the honest broker and a good conduit to make sure he has what he needs. I have a lot of contacts of my own, and a lot of people, once they read my name in the paper, started sending me their ideas. There's a whole network of people in think tanks and academia who like to give their ideas to presidential candidates."

Madeleine advised 1984 Democratic presidential candidate Walter Mondale on foreign policy issues.

Madeleine, who worked for Dukakis as a volunteer, wrote many of his speeches. She became so important to him that anyone who wanted to see him about a foreign policy issue had to arrange the meeting through her.

Dukakis lost his election to President Reagan's vice president, George Bush. Madeleine made a critical contact during the campaign, as she has so often in her career. Bill Clinton, the then governor of Arkansas, helped Dukakis with his speechmaking. Three years later, in 1991, Clinton attended one of Madeleine's political dinner seminars and they chatted. It was not until the annual dinner of the Democratic Governors Association in the spring of 1992 that the two became closer and realized they had similar ideas on how to guide the foreign policy of the United States.

Madeleine had not been idle since Dukakis's 1988 loss. The year after the election, she became president of the Center for National Policy, a nonprofit Democratic research institute. This new job made her even more prominent in Democratic circles. Her old mentor, Edmund Muskie, before his death, expressed the opinion that, were the Democrats to regain control of the White House, Madeleine should be considered for the position of national security adviser or even secretary of state. "If we're going to make these things unisexual, then Madeleine ought to be at the head of the line. She has the ability. She is as credible, as on top of emerging foreign policy, as anyone I know," Muskie said.

Madeleine first met Bill Clinton while working as a foreign policy advisor for the 1988 Democratic presidential candidate Michael Dukakis (left).

Madeleine's influence on Capitol Hill was also increasing. A spokesperson for the Senate Foreign Relations Committee said in 1991 that she was "one of the people we turn to for advice and perspective." She conducted meetings at the Capitol at which leaders of Eastern European countries and other nations met with members of Congress and their senior aides. One such assignment particularly close to her heart was the opportunity to assist her native country's transition to democracy. When playwright, human-rights campaigner, and recently elected Czechoslovakian president Vaclav Havel visited Washington in 1990, he recruited her as his interpreter. They soon became close friends.

Madeleine also continued teaching at Georgetown University's School of Foreign Service, where she was popular with her students. "She was like a Pied Piper," said the dean who hired her. "Students flocked to her." By 1993, she had won four "Teacher of the Year" awards, a record number for the university, according to a news account that attributed her success as an educator to "her approachability and knack for presenting complicated issues in plain language."

Madeleine had also started developing a widely respected reputation among political scientists. In addition to three books, among them *The Soviet Diplomatic Service: Profile of an Elite*, Madeleine wrote book chapters and articles for professional journals. She also was a trustee of the Black Student Fund, the Democratic Forum, Wellesley College, and was a member of the boards of directors of the Washington Urban League and the Atlantic Council. She had been a member of the Council on Foreign Relations, the Czechoslovak Society for Arts and Sciences, the American Association for the Advancement of Slavic Studies, the executive committee of District of Columbia Citizens for Better Public Education, and several other groups. She also continued mastering languages, learning to read and speak Russian and Polish, in addition to English, Czech, and French.

Madeleine worked with the Democratic National Committee to formulate the party's 1992 platform. Later in the campaign, she collaborated with Warren Christopher, Anthony Lake and Samuel R. Berger. The four worked as a team to develop foreign policy position papers for Bill Clinton, who won the Democratic nomination for president that summer.

Bill Clinton went on to be elected president in 1992. It was a surprising development, because most observers thought the American victory in the 1990-1991 Gulf War with Iraq had assured President Bush's reelection. Clinton had little foreign policy experience and knew he needed trusted and talented advisors in that field. Madeleine soon became one of the people he came to rely on. He decided he wanted her in an important position in his administration.

At a press conference on December 22, 1992, president-elect Clinton introduced Madeleine as his choice to be America's ambassador to the United Nations. He also named Warren Christopher, Anthony Lake and Samuel Berger to his foreign policy team. Madeleine said at the press conference: "As a result of the generous spirit of the American people, our family had the privilege of growing up as free Americans. You can therefore understand how proud I will be to sit at the United Nations behind the nameplate that says 'United States of America.'"

Long-time *Washington Post* columnist Mary McGrory approved Madeleine's selection. In a December 29, 1992, column she described Madeleine as "an intellectual . . . with a heart" and added, "She is precisely the kind of woman everyone wished could have been in the room when the men were making their disastrous decisions about [the] Vietnam [War]."

At her confirmation hearing, held before the Senate Foreign Relations Committee on January 21, 1993, Madeleine announced clearly her vision of the role the United Nations should play in the future. "I am firmly convinced that today we are witnessing the best chance for fulfilling the United Nations' original mission." She reminded the senators that the UN mission statement calls upon the institution "to save succeeding generations from the scourge of war, to reaffirm faith in fundamental human rights, to establish conditions under which justice and respect for international law can be maintained, and to promote social progress and better standards of life in larger freedom. We not only need to fulfill their dreams but also to make this international organization face the challenges of the next century," she said. "And if we do not do it today, we may not have another opportunity."

Not quite a month later, on January 27, 1993, the Senate unanimously confirmed Madeleine's nomination. She was sworn into office the next day. President Clinton announced that he would bestow cabinet officer rank to the position, just as President Reagan had done for Jeane J. Kirkpatrick, the first female U.S. Ambassador to the world body.

Chapter Six

Fourteen Suits and a Skirt

As the UN ambassador, Madeleine became a member of the diplomatic corps, which has been called the last bastion of old-boy male chauvinism in the federal government. Traditionally run by well-to-do men with family connections to power, the diplomats have frowned on women seeking important jobs in their ranks. Madeleine, however, soon proved to any doubters that she had plenty of experience as a woman who had worked her way up in this traditional group that did not give up its powers easily.

One of the ways Madeleine dealt with old attitudes was with humor. She told friends that someday she would write a book about serving on the Security Council, the leadership body of the United Nations. The book would be called *Fourteen Suits and a Skirt*, she laughed. On one Valentine's Day she put candy in red gift bags on the empty chairs of the fourteen other council members. Each bag contained a note saying how proud she was "to sit with fourteen handsome young men." She described her job during a speech at one reception as having been "sent here by my government to eat." And she began another speech in Miami by saying, "I was originally to speak . . . at the Seaquarium event on a program that included Flipper the dolphin and Lolita the killer whale. At the UN, I have dealt with the Iraqis, the Iranians, the Cubans, the Libyans, and the North Koreans. But I know better than to compete for attention with a marine mammal."

Madeleine did not joke about the situation of the other women at the UN. She worked especially hard to forge closer ties with the few women ambassadors among the 185 permanent representatives, and often expressed her determination to increase their numbers.

Madeleine loved her new job. One observer agreed, adding that she was kind and hospitable and had a "strong strain of maternal solicitude, and is universally known as a good soul." Someone else who knew her said, "What I've always found striking about Madeleine is her humanity, her true concern for individuals and their welfare." She's been described as "a person of passionate temper" and "fiercely, emotionally proud" to be representing the U.S. at the UN. People liked her willingness to speak out, her ability to understand the complicated issues that came before the UN, and her willingness to both lead and to listen.

There were a few perks. Her official title was "ambassador extraordinary and plenipotentiary." She had a staff of one hundred and a $27,000 a month apartment suite at the top of the Waldorf Towers Hotel in New York City.

The job involved more than just making speeches and meeting with other ambassadors—though she spent a lot of time doing that. She was a member of President Clinton's cabinet, the group of people who head all the departments. She was also a member of the National Security Council, where she had worked fifteen years earlier as a staff member. As a key presidential adviser on foreign policy, she attended a gathering every two weeks known as the "principals meeting," along with the director of the Central Intelligence Agency, secretaries of defense and state, and the National Security adviser.

With all these meetings in the capital, Madeleine found herself shuttling between the UN headquarters in New York City and Washington as often as five times a week. When the weather was good, she took the plane; when it was bad, she rode the train. Sometimes she even drove. And when she absolutely could not leave New York, she participated in meetings by teleconference.

Because of her busy schedule, Madeleine disliked long-windedness in speakers and meetings—and she wasn't afraid to say so. In the early months of the Clinton administration, meetings, especially those about foreign policy, tended to last a long time. Everyone tried to get an opportunity to express his or her views. At one teleconference with the White House, the topic was the proper role of the United States in the worsening Bosnian crisis. She sat patiently until finally becoming exasperated at the longwinded discussion between National Security Adviser Anthony Lake and the State Department diplomats. "Gentlemen," the exasperated Madeleine finally said, "It's nice to think about all these things we hope to do or wish we could do. But you better start figuring out what we're going to do and whether we're going to send in troops to enforce a cease-fire." The discussion quickly got back on track.

Madeleine was not modest about her new power. "The people I work with appreciate the fact that I'm plugged into Washington. I'm in the inner circle. I'm involved in everything." She didn't hesitate to express her views in public as well as in private, and her public relations skills stood her in good stead. In her almost four years at the UN, she acted on the president's orders to help put U.S. policy in place. She appeared on countless television news programs to explain U.S. policy, worked on Capitol Hill to gain congressional acceptance of a more streamlined and efficient UN, gave speeches all over the United States, and was written about in most major newspapers and magazines around the world.

Being ambassador was hard work. Every dinner was a business meeting with other ambassadors. She visited the home country of every Security Council member and made

As Ambassador to the UN, Madeleine worked with both Secretary General Boutros Boutros-Ghali (right) and U.S. Secretary of Defense William Perry.

sure that each ambassador introduced her to his own foreign minister—all to make friends for the critical moments that were sure to come.

She did not always win friends with her tactics. Sometimes she created controversy. Acting on orders from President Clinton, she led the successful effort to fire UN Secretary-General Boutros Boutros-Ghali. Once, when the Chinese representative could not vote on an anti-Cuba statement until he received instructions from his government, she kept the Security Council in session until 4 a.m. until he received permission to vote. Another time, when the British representative tried to get approval for partly lifting economic sanctions on Serbia, Madeleine walked out of the room.

Madeleine also developed a reputation for ignoring bureaucratic procedures. She often bypassed assistant secretaries back in Washington and telephoned State Department experts to get advice on a foreign country. When she found herself at odds with fellow Security Council members, she would occasionally head for the nearest phone booth, call their foreign ministers back in the members' capital, and demand that they tell their own ambassadors to vote differently.

Madeleine's dealing with the conflict over economic sanctions against Iraq is a good example of how she operated within, and without, the world body.

Iraq invaded its neighbor Kuwait in 1990 and had been forced out by an army commanded by the United States. The UN had imposed a trade embargo against Iraq. This meant no country could do business with Iraq. The goal of the embargo was to force Iraq to give up its missiles and its stocks of chemical and biological weapons, to stop it from threatening its neighbors, and to return any prisoners they still held. But Iraqi dictator Saddam Hussein was slow to respond to the embargo and complained of it often.

Madeleine, in agreement with President Clinton, was determined to keep the embargo in place. In 1994, when France, Russia and China began pushing to have the embargo relaxed, Madeleine flew to the other capitals of the

Security Council states and showed the leaders of those nations secret photos of the weapons Saddam Hussein was hiding. When she returned to New York, the motion to relieve the sanctions was dropped. When asked about the effect of the embargo on Iraqi children, she replied, "Those sanctions have worked . . . In imposing sanctions, we had no wish to hurt the Iraqi people. We exempted food and medicine and offered Saddam Hussein a chance to sell oil to buy additional humanitarian supplies." The fact he refused to meet the terms of the embargo was his responsibility, she insisted.

Madeleine was especially proud of persuading the UN to support the threatened U.S. invasion of Haiti. The U.S. wanted to remove the military officers who had overthrown the democratically elected president. "They have created a puppet show and called it a government," she said of the military dictators during a 1994 UN Security Council meeting. She then issued an ultimatum to the Haitian officers: "You can depart voluntarily and soon, or you can depart involuntarily and soon."

Her insistence on military action in Haiti led to a show-down with the cautious General Colin Powell, who at the time was still chairman of the Joint Chiefs. His response to her pressure was dramatic: "I thought I would have an aneurysm. American GIs were not toy soldiers to be moved around on some sort of global gameboard," he wrote in his memoirs.

Madeleine did not apologize for threatening the use of the American army. After the American negotiators, including General Powell, persuaded the dictators to leave and American soldiers moved in to keep the peace, Madeleine attended the swearing in ceremony for Jean-Bertrand Aristide, the elected president. She later told an interviewer: "As I looked around the crowd, I could not help but think that many of those cheering people would have ended up on leaky rafts headed for our shores if we, and the UN, had not acted to restore democracy."

There are sometimes limits to what Madeleine's leadership in the UN, and the American Army in the field, could accomplish. The war-wracked, East African nation of Somalia seemed to be a perfect place for military intervention. The plan was for American soldiers to stop the fighting long enough for the farmers to grow crops and feed the people. Madeleine even flew into Mogadishu, the capital of Somalia, and rode through the city in an armored personnel carrier wearing a flak jacket. She said that she had come to see for herself whether the "petty tyrants and defiant war lords" who were waging the civil war could be stopped.

Her enthusiasm for armed intervention in Somalia was diminished, however, when American soldiers were killed trying to stop the fighting. It was a sobering experience for her. She soon began talking about her new "do-ability doctrine," in which the United States would avoid committing to only one strategy in each situation. Somalia was not

General Colin Powell felt that Madeleine was too quick to suggest using U.S. troops to restore democracy in Haiti.

Iraq, where military intervention had worked. Each problem needed to be treated separately, with the proper solution applied.

The civil war in Bosnia, part of the former nation of Yugoslavia, had already killed thousands of people and made many more thousands homeless before the Clinton Administration came to power. Soon after coming to the UN, Madeleine sent President Clinton a memo urging him to begin air strikes against the Bosnian Serbs' heavy weapons. She argued forcibly that the Bosnian Serbs were the cause of the conflict and had to be stopped if peace was to have a chance.

To emphasize her point, and to show the world how much the U.S. cared about bringing peace to the area, she toured the ravaged Bosnian capital city of Sarajevo wearing a helmet and body armor.

Being an ambassador who traveled to war-torn areas of the world was sometimes risky. In March of 1996, as she toured the ruined Croatian city of Vukovar, Madeleine found herself the target of an angry Serbian mob, who claimed ownership of the city. As protesters yelled obscenities and chanted "This is Serbia," she retreated slowly to her bus. Her motorcade drove off in a hail of stones.

Ironically, the incident in Vukovar illustrated her fame around the world. There were few other members of President Clinton's Cabinet who would have been recog-

Madeleine, seen here visiting U.S. peacekeeping troops, dedicated herself as UN ambassador to bringing an end to the Bosnian Civil War.

Madeleine tried to meet with citizens, such as these children, during her visit to Sarajevo during the Bosnian Civil War.

nized by a crowd of angry Serbs in a small Balkan town. The incident also illustrated her ability to conduct herself with dignity in a difficult and potentially dangerous situation. This was made more difficult because she was the only member of her party who understood that the Serbian demonstrators were shouting, "kucko, kucko," or "bitch, bitch." During the years in Belgrade, when her father was a diplomat in Yugoslavia, she had learned some Serbian.

Madeleine is remarkably at ease on such occasions. "You know what I discovered about myself that I did not know? It's that I'm not afraid," she said. "I've done what I need to for my family. My daughters are the greatest source of pride for me—but they don't really depend on me anymore. I have a great sense of freedom now."

Madeleine's persistent focus on the Bosnian conflict sometimes clashed with the message coming from the White House and from the State Department. It sometimes seemed as though she argued for a much more active role for the United States than did others in the administration. But her focus paid off when the warring groups finally agreed to attempt to settle their differences peacefully.

Madeleine's talent for pithy, strong comments was best in evidence in February of 1996 when Cuban fighter pilots shot down two unarmed planes flown by members of a group that sought to free the island nation from communist rule. Madeleine denounced the action in the Security Council. Later, when she heard that the Cuban pilots were bragging about their actions, she said, "Frankly, this is not *cojones* (Spanish for testicles), this is cowardice." President Clinton was pleased with her comment. He called it the best one-liner of his administration.

Clever put-downs were one thing. Forcing the UN to get tough with the Cubans was another. A statement originally intended to condemn Cuba and to set the stage for further punitive actions was watered down by the Chinese and Russians, two of communist Cuba's longtime allies. Finally, she was able to get the Security Council to agree to "deplore"—but not "condemn"—the action.

Madeleine's work at the UN earned her a reputation as a "hawk" (as people who are ready to use the army are often called). She is a great fan of the military. This was apparent when she donned camouflage paint in 1994 for a visit to army troops in Louisiana. She even ate the army's less-than-gourmet MREs (Meals Ready to Eat). She keeps an enormous Marine Corps knife on her desk.

Her tough ideas about foreign policy developed over many years, although her childhood experiences in war-torn Europe probably influenced her thinking most. She thinks the Vietnam War formed the foreign policy views of most of her generation, and that this makes them overly cautious about using military power, because of their fear of being sucked into another tragic war. While acknowledging the lessons of Vietnam, she considers the Munich Agreement as the single biggest influence on her philosophy about international relations. In the Munich Agreement the British and French gave control of her native Czechoslovakia to Nazi Germany in a vain attempt to avoid war. Madeleine believes force and the threat of force must be used carefully, but it must be a viable alternative if a country hopes to have an effective foreign policy.

This can seem to be a complicated and contradictory view of the military's role in a modern democracy. Because of it, Madeleine has sometimes been accused of inconsistency. She admits to changing her mind on some positions, partly because of the U.S. experience in Somalia. She sometimes reminds critics that her "do-ability" doctrine can mean doing nothing.

To those Americans, however, who simply want the U.S. to stay out of other countries because intervention costs money and sometimes the lives of American soldiers, she says: "Yes, it costs money to help keep peace around the world. But . . . the most expensive peacekeeping mission is a bargain compared to the least expensive war—not just because it costs fewer dollars, but because it costs fewer lives and creates fewer refugees and orphans, and because it plants the seeds of future reconciliation, not future revenge."

Chapter Seven

Reaching the Top

On the Sunday before the presidential election of November 1996, in which President Clinton was coasting to an easy victory over Senator Bob Dole, Madeleine's old friend Senator Patrick Leahy of Vermont was visiting her at her Waldorf Towers apartment in New York. They both knew that Secretary of State Warren Christopher had told the president he was planning to resign and return to his law practice in Los Angeles. Leahy had a question for Madeleine. What would she do if she got Christopher's job?

Most other Washington insiders would have pretended modesty and declined to answer. It is usually not wise to let your ambition be too clearly revealed in that highly competitive city. But Madeleine was Madeleine, and she talked for a long time about how she saw the problems of the world and what the United States' role should be in it. Later that night Leahy wrote in his diary, "This country would be well served if she [Madeleine] were the next secretary of state."

Madeleine had been aware since she had become UN ambassador that she might have the opportunity to replace Secretary of State Christopher. She never hid her excitement at the prospect. The job was considered to be the very top role a diplomat could ever achieve—and a woman had never held it. When she received word that the president had been reelected, she was at the Security Council. That did not keep her from doing the Macarena, the popular dance that had her swaying and swinging her arms.

From the beginning, her chances to win the job of secretary of state were good. Madeleine frequently joked that she had always treated CNN, the all-news cable television network, as the 16th member of the Security Council, always making herself available for interviews, and had generally proved to be the administration's best foreign policy salesperson. She shared the president's concern that the administration put on the best possible appearance in public. Mr. Clinton liked grand gestures, and being a woman would not hurt her chances. It would be an achievement for him to name the first female secretary of state.

She had also impressed the president with the passion of her views on Bosnia, inspiring him to take a tougher stance toward the Serbs, leading to the Dayton peace agreement that ended the Bosnian Civil War. It was her advocacy of a strong stand in Bosnia, and her facing-down of the Iraqis in the UN, that had started the president thinking about her as a potential secretary of state.

For years the talk in Washington had been that her blunt support of the president, especially compared to the endless caution of Secretary Christopher, had made her a logical candidate. One administration official had even said, "She is hot around here." Another had called her "a star," and a third "a crown jewel."

Madeleine had worked to win important allies, such as Hillary Clinton, with whom she had spent a day at the UN women's conference in Beijing, the capital of China, in September 1995. She had also guided her around Prague in July of 1996 and worked to maintain her contact with the influential first lady. "She advises Mrs. Clinton on international stuff, sends her memos and material. Madeleine's great champion for this job [secretary of state] was Mrs. Clinton," said one insider.

A major potential obstacle in the Senate was Republican Senator Jesse Helms, the very conservative chairman of the Senate Foreign Relations Committee, which would have to approve her nomination. But she had wisely been "courting" him for several years. Senator Helms liked her because she was so strong an opponent of communist governments around the world. He was also delighted that she had led the effort to fire Boutros Boutros-Ghali as secretary-general of the UN, and he loved her "cojones" comment about the Cuban pilots.

Madeleine charmed the Republican chairman of the Senate Foreign Relations Committee, Senator Jesse Helms.

Madeleine made sure to return Helms' admiration. In 1995 she had appeared with him at a meeting in Raleigh, the capitol of the senator's home state of North Carolina, to talk about the United Nations. Soon after the 1996 election, she asked him to introduce her to a luncheon in North Carolina. After the lunch, Senator Helms draped his napkin over his arm like a waiter, grabbed the dessert tray from the center of the table, and walked around to where Madeleine was sitting. "Madame Ambassador, may I serve you some dessert?" he said with a bow. By the time he escorted her to the airport that evening, they looked as though they were on a date.

There were people both in and out of the White House, however, who did not think Madeleine was the best candidate for secretary of state. Her opponents in the White House argued that she was not "serious" enough. They said she did not have the experience to manage a department that had embassies all over the world. They also did not think she was smart enough to figure out what U.S. foreign policy should be.

As Mr. Clinton was making his cabinet decisions, White House aides opposed to Madeleine put out the word that she had fallen to the "second tier"—meaning that she would be considered only if all the higher-ranked candidates failed the president's tests. "That was like 'Kazaam!'" said Maryland Senator Barbara Mikulski, a close friend of Madeleine's.

"It was an insult to all of us. And it gave us the opportunity to launch a full-court press."

Senator Mikulski lobbied for Hillary Clinton's support over a veggie-burger lunch at the White House "mess" (cafeteria). Connecticut Representative Barbara Kennelly called Vice President Gore to push for Madeleine's nomination. This was a wise move. Vice President Gore was influential in the White House, and Madeleine had always been his backup choice. He wanted to make sure that the women who supported the president would support him when he ran for president in the year 2000. He began to look at Madeleine more favorably after the phone conversation.

Madeleine herself had to move carefully during this period. Her allies asked feminist groups to keep quiet this time. "Don't turn her into a quota," one told them.

During these nervous days, Madeleine ran into Health and Human Services Secretary Donna Shalala outside the White House mess. "Whadda ya hear?" Madeleine asked in a whisper. "Keep your head down and stay cool," Shalala whispered back. Madeleine nodded and continued to keep her "fingerprints" carefully off any campaign on her behalf.

President Clinton finally called, but only to chat. A few days later, Madeleine had a "heads-up"—advance warning—from incoming chief of staff Erskine Bowles that good news might be on the way. According to an aide, Albright and her staff chatted nervously, and that night, in her Georgetown home, the ambassador slept fitfully. The next day, December 5, 1996, the president called to offer her the job of secretary of state.

After the president's call, Madeleine did one last bit of discreet lobbying. She knew that even with Senator Helms in her camp she still had to get the approval of the full Senate, which was controlled by the Republicans, the opposition party. So, at a formal dinner they were both attending, she asked Washington insider and former Reagan administration appointee Kenneth Duberstein how to approach the new Republican senators on the Foreign Relations Committee. His answer was to sit down with them for one-on-one talks.

Madeleine began visiting the senators in their office, one at a time. Eventually, she had the support of everyone on the committee. By the time the senators voted, on January 22, 1997, she was back in her UN office, packing everything in boxes and watching the Senate vote on her nomination on C-Span, the cable channel that carries the debates and votes in Congress. When the vote was announced, she fell back in her chair, threw her arms over her head, and let out a whoop. It was 99 to 0.

Madeleine was sworn in the next day in a ceremony in the Oval Office of the White House. Cleverly combining a pointed remark about her gender and a compliment to her predecessor, she turned to Warren Christopher early in the

As her daughters and President Clinton look on, Madeleine is sworn in as the first female secretary of state.

ceremony and said, "I can only hope that my heels can fill your shoes."

In his comments, the president said Madeleine's gender "had nothing to do with her getting the job." But he also said, smiling: "Am I proud that I got a chance to appoint the first woman secretary of state? You bet I am. My mamma's smiling down at me right now."

Madeleine's proud children were in the audience, smiling up at her. "Of course, all three of us are thrilled for our mom," said her daughter Anne. "We went to the Senate for her confirmation hearings, to the Capitol for the presidential inauguration and to the White House for her swearing in. But we've been proud of her all along . . . She's going to conduct the foreign policy of the United States as it should be conducted. She's a tough, gutsy lady, and she's extremely talented."

Josef and Mandula did not live to see their daughter's proud moment. Josef had died in 1977 and Mandula had died in 1989. But Madeleine liked to say that she knew they, too, were looking down from heaven and smiling.

Chapter Eight

Madam Secretary

The revelation of Madeleine's Jewish heritage happened just as she achieved the goal that she had worked for her entire life. The story was broken in December 1996 by Arab newspapers that expressed the concern that she would favor the Jewish state of Israel in the long-running conflict between that country and its Arab neighbors.

Madeleine had earlier denied the stories, but now announced that she had accepted that her family heritage was Jewish. Reporters and other commentators wondered if she had always known the truth but had kept it secret in order to further her career. Madeleine strongly denied this accusation. She repeated that she had been raised as a Catholic and had always thought of herself as Catholic. She had been a young child during World War II and had never been told the extent her family was decimated by the Nazis. These were points that the people who had known her then agreed were true.

When asked if the revelations about her family's Jewish

roots and their suffering during the Holocaust might change the way she looked at the world, Madeleine told reporters, "All you have to do is read my speeches or talk to my friends to know that I have always believed the Holocaust to be one of the greatest horrors of history. "And," she had added, "I have to say that I'm very proud of the way I lived my life. I have comported myself [as one] who had known what it's like to be a victim of totalitarianism."

Even the controversy over her ancestry could not destroy the thrill of becoming the first female secretary of state. When one interviewer asked if she ever pinched herself to see if she was dreaming, Madeleine replied, "Every morning. Somebody said to me early on, 'Do you realize that you have Thomas Jefferson's job?' A little awe there."

If Madeleine needed one more reminder that she had arrived at the peak of a formerly all-male part of the United States government, she got it when she moved into her new office. The gray marble bathroom was outfitted "for the boys," she said, with suit racks and a long column of small, thin sock drawers. To make it more "homey," she brought in her pictures and awards, and her Harlem Globetrotters jersey and autographed basketball.

Madeleine also moved quickly to let everyone know she was in charge. Former Secretary of State Christopher had not been a strong administrator, and some of the State Department's traditional decision-making powers had been taken over by other departments. She acted quickly to move

Madeleine (with Palestinian leader Yasir Arafat) knows that the long conflict in the mid-east will challenge her as secretary of state.

several important people into her office, including an undersecretary from the Commerce Department to become her new undersecretary for economic affairs.

Madeleine also quickly proved her toughness. Each morning she met with her assistants to hear brief reports on the world's "hot spots." When someone "leaked" to the press—revealed without permission—the results of one of these meetings at which China policy had been discussed, she gathered all the top officials and warned them about keeping necessary secrets. She also made it clear that people caught leaking information would be fired. Within the hour, the phones were ringing throughout the building. The message was always the same. Madeleine was a tough boss.

Madeleine let the world know that the second half of the Clinton administration would have a strong and decisive foreign policy. She also let it be known, as she had while serving as ambassador, that America would make its power felt in the world. "I would never recommend that the president of the U.S. use force lightly," she said. America should use force where it can achieve realistic goals. The problem is to decide where those places are.

Madeleine knows there are plenty of troubled areas, and perplexing questions, around the world. The NATO alliance, created to withstand the expansion of the now-defunct Soviet Union, will be expanded to include countries from the old Soviet block. Which nations will be added and when promises to be a long standing issue. What is going to happen in Russia, struggling to survive after the collapse of the Soviet Union? The continuing violence in Bosnia, and the responsibility to bring the leaders of past atrocities to justice, continues to create controversy within Europe and the United States. The Middle East conflict between Israel and Palestine has been a constant issue since the late 1940s and still causes almost weekly bloodshed. Iraq and Iran are still attempting to create chaos in various parts of the globe.

The list is long, and in all of these situations, Madeleine's goal is to get as many countries as possible to accept international law and agreements, and to settle their differences peacefully.

Madeleine continues her lifelong habits of hard work and maintaining organization. She rises before dawn and stays up late. She reads all the necessary materials thoroughly before meetings and rehearses her pointed, newsworthy public comments so they sound unrehearsed. "I do not believe that things happen accidentally," she says. "I believe you earn them."

It is not enough to be the highest-ranking woman in the history of the executive branch of the government. She wants to be a secretary of state unlike any before her. But she is not stuffy and is not afraid for the public to know that even as secretary of state there will be shopping trips when she visits foreign capitals. She's also not afraid to have a good time in other ways. She created a small sensation in New York City in May 1997 when she went nightclubbing with her friend and Czech president Vaclav Havel and Havel's friend rock-and-roll musician Lou Reed. Havel had long been a fan of Reed's music. When he and his wife arrived with Reed at a nightclub to hear a concert by John Zorn, many of the guests were surprised when Madeleine joined them. The club's owner later told a reporter that "Albright was talking a little too loudly to Havel and Zorn grabbed a microphone and said, 'Would everyone up in the balcony please be quiet and listen to the music.' And they did. It was a great concert."

Los Angeles is another favorite place for Madeleine to visit because it is the home of her friend, singer and actor Barbra Streisand. Madeleine and Barbra met at a Hollywood Women's Political Caucus meeting in early 1993. "We just became instant friends," Streisand says. "We talk about everything: love, relationships, a lot of politics." They go shopping for antiques together, talk often on the phone, and try to get together whenever they're in the same city.

Both women have busy schedules, but they try to find time to spend together. On one day, for example, Madeleine awoke aboard the aircraft carrier *Constellation*, which was sailing in the Pacific when she made an official visit. She had breakfast with the officers, flew back to San Diego in a tiny propeller plane, gave a speech at a luncheon in her honor, made calls back to New York and Washington, drove to Los Angeles, attended a reception with Korean-Americans, and gave two interviews and a news conference. At

10:30 that night, Barbra called. She wanted to show off her new house. Madeleine, although weary, went off to dinner and a house tour with Barbra.

Madeleine has a farm in Virginia that provides a way to relax and escape the limelight. The house is decorated in a cow motif, with bovine potholders and figurines adorning the kitchen where she cooks. Madeleine escapes there as often as possible.

There is no escape, though, from the special situation that a woman in such an important position inevitably receives. When should she be tough and hard, soft and gentle?

Then there are the questions that a divorced man in her position probably would never be asked. Would she consider remarriage? Her answer to this question comes without hesitation. "There's no way, unless I were married to some truly unusual man who had a whole life of his own, that I could possibly be married," she says. "And there are not a lot of them around." She resents being asked about it. "There are lots of questions about women that don't come up for men, like 'How do you stand being alone?'" she says. She also gets particularly irritated when reporters write about her looks.

Madeleine is the first to admit, however, that these are trifling irritations in the face of the opportunity she now has to help shape American foreign policy. Much as her father had been before her, Madeleine is a patriot deeply concerned about the future of her country and of the peoples in the world who look to the United States for leadership.

On June 5, 1997, Madeleine stood before the assembled graduates, parents, and teachers of Harvard University to give the commencement address. It would be no ordinary commencement address. She would be sharing with the world her ideas on how the United States should deal with the rest of the world, and she would be doing it in the shadow of one of her most illustrious predecessors, George Marshall. He had helped to lead the United States and its allies to victory in World War II and then, here in Harvard Yard, had proposed a plan to help lift Europe from the ruins of war.

". . . On this day fifty years ago," she began, "Secretary of State George Marshall . . . spoke to a class enriched by many who had fought for freedom, and deprived of many who had fought for freedom and died. . . . Secretary Marshall did not adorn his rhetoric with high-flown phrases, saying only that it would be logical for America to help restore normal economic health to the world, without which there could be no political stability and no assured peace. . . . After the devastation of World War II and the soul-withering horror of the Holocaust . . . the message . . . from the White House, from both parties on Capitol Hill, and from people across our country who donated millions in relief cash, clothing and food was that this time, America would not turn inward; America would lead."

Today, Madeleine acknowledged, the world was not like

it was in Marshall's day. The threat of communism was gone, but many other threats remained—nuclear weapons in the wrong hands, terrorism, environmental damage, the spread of disease, deadly ethnic conflict. "To defend against these threats," she said, "we must take advantage of the historic opportunity that now exists to bring the world together in an international system based on democracy, open markets, law and a commitment to peace.... Let every nation acknowledge today the opportunity to be part of an international system based on democratic principles available to all."

She was speaking now as an immigrant as well as secretary of state. "This was not the case fifty years ago," she noted sadly. "Then, my father's boss, Jan Masaryk, foreign minister of what was then Czechoslovakia, was told by [the Soviet dictator, Joseph] Stalin in Moscow that his country must not participate in the Marshall Plan . . . . Masaryk said it was at that moment that he understood he was employed by a government no longer sovereign in its own land. Today, there is no Stalin."

She urged the United States and the other wealthy nations of the world to help the poor countries of Africa, Asia, and Latin America build their economies and their democratic governments. But whether we provided aid to such countries or merely sought to trade with them, they must also be required to play by the rules. Communist North Korea should prove that its nuclear program was not a threat to other nations. China should follow international rules. NATO will invite new members from Eastern Europe, formerly under the domination of the Soviet Union, to join. And in Bosnia, the Dayton Peace Accords (which she had been so instrumental in bringing about) were the "map" to achieve a permanent peace between the Bosnian Muslims, Croats, and Serbs.

The issue of Bosnia that had been such a concern of hers during her tenure at the UN remained unsettled. The woman who had just learned for certain that many of her family had died in the Holocaust was determined to bring the killers in Bosnia to justice through an international war crimes tribunal. "The majority of Bosnia killings occurred not in battle, but in markets, streets and playgrounds, where men and women like you and me, and boys and girls like those we know, were abused or murdered—not because of anything they had done, but simply for who they were. We all have a stake in establishing a precedent that will deter future atrocities, in holding accountable the perpetrators of ethnic cleansing, and in seeing that those who consider rape just another tactic of war answer for their crimes.

"While in Sarajevo, I visited a playground in the area once known as 'sniper's alley,' where many Bosnians had earlier been killed because of ethnic hate. But this past weekend, the children were playing there without regard to whether the child in the next swing was Muslim, Serb, or Croat. They thanked America for helping to fix their swings,

Madeleine receives an honorary degree from Harvard, June 5, 1997.

and asked me to place in the soil a plant which they promised to nourish and tend.

"I can still remember in England, during the war, sitting in the bomb shelter, singing away the fear and thanking God for America's help. I can still remember, after the war and after the communist takeover in Prague, arriving here in the United States, where I wanted only to be accepted and to make my parents and my new country proud.

"Because my parents fled in time, I escaped Hitler. To our shared and constant sorrow, millions did not. Because of America's generosity, I escaped Stalin. Millions did not. I have been privileged to live my life in freedom. Millions have still never had that opportunity. It may be hard for you, who have no memory of that time 50 years ago, to understand. But it is necessary that you try to understand.

"We have a responsibility...not to be prisoners of history, but to shape history...and to build with others a global network of purpose and law that will protect our citizens, defend our interests, preserve our values, and bequeath to future generations a legacy as proud as the one we honor today."

Looking out over the people gathered to hear her, she finished on a heartfelt note. "To that mission, I pledge my own best efforts and summon yours." The young people listening to her would be moving out into a complicated and sometimes dangerous world—and she wanted to make it as safe as possible for them.

The little girl who had escaped the Nazis and hidden from their bombs, who had escaped the communists, come to the United States and proved what an energetic and determined woman could do for her country and her family, would now take the lead in organizing the world for peace. Her challenge to the graduates of Harvard is also her challenge to America. The story of Madeleine Korbel Albright's life suggests that she has the personal qualities needed to successfully carry this challenge forward.

Timeline

May 15, 1937:	Madeleine Korbel born to Josef and Mandula Korbel in Prague, Czechoslovakia.
1939:	Nazis take over government of Czechoslovakia. Madeleine's family flees to London.
1945:	Korbels return home and discover entire family has been murdered by Nazis. Madeleine is not told.
1948:	Korbels flee to London and New York to escape communist government in Prague
1949:	Korbels move to Colorado and Josef takes teaching position at University of Denver
1951:	Madeleine starts high school at Kent Denver School.
1955:	Madeleine graduates from Kent Denver and enters Wellesley College.
1959:	Madeleine graduates from Wellesley and marries Joseph Albright.
1961:	Joe goes to work for "Newsday" on Long Island, outside New York City. Madeleine gives birth to twins Alice and Anne. Enrolls in graduate political science program at Columbia University.
1967:	Gives birth to daughter Katherine
1968:	Earns masters degree in political science. Begins doctoral dissertation on Czechoslovakian democracy movement. Joe becomes head of "Newsday's" Washington bureau and family moves to nation's capital.

1972:	Becomes fundraiser for Senator Edmund Muskie's presidential campaign
1976:	Awarded Ph.D. in political science. Joins Senator Muskie's staff.
1977:	Josef Korbel dies
1978:	Madeleine joins staff of President Carter's National Security Council.
1981:	Leaves government when Ronald Reagan is elected. Joins staff of Center for Strategic and International Studies. Wins fellowship at Woodrow Wilson Center.
1982:	Appointed professor of international relations at Georgetown University in Washington and director of the Women in Foreign Service Program. Continues there until 1993. Divorces Joe.
1984:	Foreign policy coordinator for Mondale presidential campaign. Joins National Democratic Institute for International Affairs.
1988:	Becomes foreign policy coordinator for Dukakis presidential campaign.
1989:	Becomes president of Center For National Policy. Mandula Korbel dies.
1992:	Madeleine works with Democratic National Committee to formulate party's platform in upcoming presidential election. Assists Clinton campaign in formulating foreign policy. Nominated by Clinton as next ambassador to U.N.
1993-1997:	United States Ambassador to United Nations. December, 1996: Nominated as next Secretary of State by President Clinton
January, 1997:	Confirmed by United States Senate as Secretary of State.
February, 1997:	Goes online with students worldwide—first Secretary of State to do so.
June, 1997:	Speech at Harvard University outlining her vision for America's foreign relations.

Bibliography

CBS "60 Minutes", 9 February 1997

Current Biography Yearbook, 1995

D. Abraham, "Yated Neeman" newspaper, online at http:\\www.yated.com/hidher.htm

Newsweek, 16 Dec 96

Newsweek, 10 Feb 97

New York Post, 17 May 17, 1997

New York Times, 4 Feb 97

New York Times, 5 Feb 97

New York Times, 12 Feb 97

New York Times Magazine, 22 September, 1996

Time, 31 October 1994

Time, 17 Feb 97

"TownHall" chat room website: http://globe.fsl.noaa.gov/webchat/Albright/webchat.html)

Washington Post, 6 December, 1996

Index